Chatroom

A play

Enda Walsh

D1635491

Samuel French — London
www.samuelfrench-london.co.uk

CHATROOM

First presented at the Cottesloe Theatre as part of the National Theatre's Shell Connections Festival in July 2005.

Subsequently presented at the Cottesloe Theatre on 10th April 2006 with the following cast:

Laura	Naomi Bentley
Jim	Andrew Garfield
Eva	Matti Houghton
Jack	Javone Prince
Emily	Andrea Riseborough
William	Matt Smith

Directed by Anna Mackmin
Designed by Jonathan Fensom

CHARACTERS

Laura, fifteen
Jim, fifteen
Eva, fifteen
Jack, fifteen
Emily, fifteen
William, fifteen

The action of the play takes place on a bare stage.

Time — 2004

Oompa Loompa
Words and Music by Leslie Bricusse and Anthony Newley
© Copyright Taradam Music Incorporated
1970, 1971

CHATROOM

There is a movie screen US. There are six identical orange plastic seats in a row at the very front of the stage. There's a two metre gap between each seat

The Lights come up

The song "Oompa Loompa" sung by the Oompa Loompas from the film "Willy Wonka and the Chocolate Factory" is heard

During the song William, Jack, Eva, Emily and Laura, all about fifteen to sixteen years of age, enter, three from one side of the stage, two from the other, ending up in the order from L to R as they are listed above. They walk casually towards each other in a line in front of the chairs, stop, turn and face the audience. They stand there for a while and look at the audience. They then look at each other. They seem to be sizing each other up. In unison they walk towards their seats and sit down, leaving the far R one empty. This should all last one and half minutes. They sit as the Oompa Loompas' song comes to an end

Oompa Loompas (*recorded*)
        Oompa Loompa doompadee doo,
        I've got another puzzle for you.
        Oompa Loompa doompadah dee,
        If you are wise you will listen to me.

        Who do you blame when your kid is a brat,
        Pampered and spoiled like a Siamese cat?
        Blaming the kids is a lion of shame,
        You know exactly who's to blame:
        The mother and the father!

Oompa Loompa doompadee dah,
If you're not spoiled then you will go far.
You will live in happiness too,
Like the Oompa Loompa
Doompadee do.

The Lights go down on all but William and Jack

William You're depressing me now.

Jack Really?

William You see you've lost me. At the beginning I was with you. But not now. I'm a little disappointed.

Jack Sorry.

William You really think that? You've thought it over, came to an opinion, you believe that?

Jack It is popular.

William Well, so is body piercing but that isn't a good thing, is it?

Jack I suppose.

William So let's look at the facts. A single man lives in a castle in the middle of ... Where is it set again?

Jack Film or book?

William There's a difference?

Jack Both films changed some details. It doesn't really matter.

William Well in the book it's set wherever it's set — and this man lives in his big house in the middle of the town. He lives with dwarfs. Nothing wrong with that. But they're orange. Orange dwarfs with green hair.

Jack And there's only twenty of them making the world's supply of chocolate ... None of this is meant to be realistic.

William But why make them dwarfs? Why the green hair? Why make them orange in the first place? Can you see where I'm going with this?

Jack Kind of.

William What's wrong with the ordinary?

Jack It's for children. Ordinary's boring, maybe?

William Which is my original point about these children's writers! As if a little boy who shares a giant bed with his grandparents — four of them! — as if he'd ever in the real world win this extraordinary chocolate empire!

Jack (*groaning*) Yeah.

William You know in the real world it would have been that fat German boy who falls into the chocolate lake at the beginning of the tour. In the real world he's the winner.

Jack I think I might have to ...

William This is how it really ends. He falls in. His father gets these big time lawyers to sue the shit out of Willy Wonka. They look into his shady past, his very dodgy personal life with those orange midgets. He's dragged through the tabloids with paedophilia ringing in his ears. They make shit out of him! Willy Wonka is no more. He's done. He's doing twenty-five years in a high security prison being passed around his fellow prisoners like the proverbial box of Quality Street. In the outside, the Germans win, 'cause let's face it the Germans always win. The fat German kiddy ——

Jack His name is Augustus.

William Right, Augustus ... Well, he inherits everything as part of his settlement. He gets it all. And because he's a fat glutton he can't stop eating all this chocolate. The more the Oompa Loompas make the more Augustus eats. He's eighteen years old and forty stone. One day he wakes up, stretches for the television remote and dies of a massive coronary sclerosis. That is the real world. Do you understand this? Where exactly are you getting confused?

Jack It's only a children's story.

William It's a lie! What's the point? What are they telling us?

Jack What are who telling us?

William The writers! Our parents! Harry fucking Potter? In the real world he's still under the stairs. He's a thirty-year-old retard who's developed his own under-the-stairs language!

Jack The point is ...

William Yes?

Jack The point is — is that children don't want to read the true stories. What child wants to read the news?! It's just escape. It's important that we dream of other things.

William Fuck off! Life's too short. If the world is going to evolve in any way — children should be told what's really happening. Cold, clear facts ... That's what's taken us down from the trees, that's what powers economy ...

Jack A lot of these children's stories are metaphors. The writers are expressing important issues in creative ways!

William "Expressing important ... "? You see, you're depressing me again!

Jack (*to himself*) Fuck sake.

William Do you think any eight-year-old finishing reading Charlie and the Chocolate Factory thinks anything other than, "I'd love a Never-ending Gob Stopper, Grandpa!"? Listen to me, John...

Jack It's Jack.

William They're trying to keep children young! Adults. Publishers. Fucking writers. They don't want children thinking for themselves. They see children as a threat. They want to keep everything "fantasy". This J.K. Rowling woman! She is the enemy. She should be taken out. Erased. Removed. Exterminated.

A pause

Jack So that's what you're doing in a Harry Potter Chatroom? Trying to drum up some interest in an assassination attempt on J.K. Rowling?

A slight pause

William Well, are you interested?

A slight pause

Jack I can't. I have to do my geography homework.

The Lights cross-fade to Eva and Emily

Eva But I was younger then and she just came on the scene, remember?

Emily Yeah.

Eva You're six years of age and that's a critical age.

Emily Of course.

Eva And the video with her at school in her school uniform and pigtails ...

Emily She looked lovely.

Eva You wanted to be her, didn't ya?

Emily She didn't have her tits done then?

Eva That was much later.

Emily But even then they were a decent size. Certainly a B-Cup.

Eva But at six you wanted to be her. And that video — wasn't it a bit creepy — in hindsight — but that thing she was doing with her tongue — it was very sexual.

Emily We didn't notice.

Eva It wasn't for the kiddies.

Emily It was for the older boys and the daddies.

Eva She's in her school uniform with her pigtails and sticking out her tongue but it's subtle. Flicking it in and out like a little parrot.

Emily It was a bit seedy.

Eva So I'm watching that video after not seeing it since I was six — and I have to say I felt betrayed by Britney. You know how her songs and videos were all about that journey from girl to woman ...

Emily Yeah.

Eva And it sort of felt good, didn't it? Like Britney Spears was a part of your puberty.

Emily I remember having my first period and listening to *I'm Not a Girl, Not Yet a Woman* and thinking, "Thanks Britney. My sentiments exactly!"

Eva She felt like a spokeswoman.

Emily Oh, definitely.

Eva But as I watched *Hit Me Baby One More Time* and all that sexual stuff with her tongue and just how cropped that crop-top was ...

Emily Was her belly-button pierced back then?

Eva Probably.

Emily Sorry, go on.

Eva I got really angry over that betrayal. It's no longer Britney who's talking to us but some pervert record producer who's got this vision, this plan of turning every six-year-old girl in the western world into a tongue-flicking, crop-topped-belly-button-pierced temptress.

Emily Have you got your belly-button pierced?

Eva Yeah, of course.

Emily Did it hurt?

Eva It's not as bad as you hear. But anyway Britney, Britney … !

Emily Yeah, Britney.

Eva Don't you think a lot of young girls began to feel that betrayal?

Emily Both of us did.

Eva And maybe that's why her career died a slow death. She lied to us.

Emily You don't think it has to do with her music being shit?

Eva A little bit ——

Emily And that she's essentially a poor girl with no respect for money and that's why she's an unmarried mother with fluctuating weight problems.

Eva But don't you think the fans realized that they were being manipulated — that they made a stand against that pervert record producer ...

Emily Britney got burnt.

Eva Britney was thick.

Emily She made her money.

Eva She lost our respect. If I met Britney Spears tomorrow I would gently pull her to one side, place my arms around her shoulders like I'm going to hug her, move my face towards her like I'm going to kiss her — and whisper in her ear, "Britney Spears, you sold my childhood soul."

Emily Oh, that's cruel.

Eva "You sold my childhood soul." Then I'd smash her in the face.

Emily And what would Britney say?

Eva *Hit Me Baby One More Time.*

Emily Of course.

Eva (*seriously*) Her day of judgement will come when some teenage girl will stop her outside Burger King and say, "You sold my childhood soul, bitch."

Emily laughs but Eva doesn't. Pause

Emily I better go. It's been very nice talking to you, whoever you are.

Eva Can we talk some more? I had an argument with my bitch-mother and I'm feeling terrible.

Emily OK. (*Pause*) So what do you want to talk about?

Pause. Eva thinks and decides

Eva Murder.

Music

> *Jim walks on stage and stops. He faces the audience and sighs. He walks to his seat next to Laura and sits*

> *The music cuts out and the Lights cross-fade to Jim and Laura*

Jim And you really don't mind listening to this?

Laura That's what the room's all about.

Jim But you'd say if you did mind? If it was too draining, too annoying, too boring, maybe ... ?

Laura I don't mind listening.

A pause

Jim Maybe I shouldn't even be in this place. I don't know whether it's that serious yet.

Laura (*directly*) There isn't a scale of depression here. I'm here at the other end and I'm here to listen to you. If you want to talk, Jim, then talk. If you don't then don't talk.

A pause

Jim Right.

Laura Don't be nervous.

Jim I'll talk then.

Laura OK.

A pause

Jim I'm a Roman Catholic — and it's last Easter — and ahhh — and every year our parish does a big Passion play in our local church. My mother's very active in the church. She's the Virgin Mary.

Laura Which would make you Jesus Christ.

Jim In the Passion play she's the Virgin Mary.

Laura I understand.

Jim And my whole family get involved. I've got three older brothers and they're Roman soldiers. They're very broad — not like me — and they look the part. One year my brother Derek went too heavy on Jesus and actually popped his knee right open. It was a mess. But anyway, this year and my mother runs into my bedroom with her "terrific news". She's building it up like she's going to tell me that I'm going to get a stab at playing a centurion — until she tells me — they want me to play John.

Laura Well, John's a great part.

Jim Yeah, but he's a bit gay.

Laura How do you mean?

Jim I've got nothing against gay people.

Laura St John was gay?

Jim Historically speaking, he probably wasn't gay. But in our parish it's always the slightly effeminate boys who get to play John.

Laura OK.

Jim Like I say — I've got nothing against gays. I respect the gay community. They're tough, they know their own mind, they stand out and they don't care, you know. I respect them. But I'm not like that at all. I'm just a sap with no bottle who knows nothing. I'm not interesting enough to play the gay icon that is St John. In a million years I could never get away with those lime robes.

Laura Lime?

Jim It's sort of an unspoken thing in the parish. It's a bit weird.

Laura Right, carry on.

Jim We do a few rehearsals with my mother as the Virgin Mary and I've got to get emotional when Jesus is dying on the cross and he says to Mary, "Woman behold your son" while looking over at me. And I'm supposed to break down at that point because I know that

Jesus is just about to croak it but I'm getting very nervous because basically I'm a terrible actor and I'm all blocked up.

Laura Emotionally blocked?

Jim Exactly.

Laura Right.

Jim So I tell my mother I want to drop out of the play. I say it quiet so the others can't hear but she starts screaming at me and saying how typical it was — and did I have a backbone? — and why was I such a coward? — and why wasn't I like my older brothers — and all this shit. And then she says I'm like my dad. But what would I know? I haven't seen my dad since I was six — but she starts shouting, "You're just like your dad, Jim!" — "Just like your dad walking out on things! Walking out on me! Gutless!" I mean, I hate her just then. Why did she have to bring up my dad in front of all of those people like that. Why? So the following night is the Passion play proper and I'm kneeling and looking up at Jesus. He's doing a wonderful job dying on the cross, this guy called Nick Lawson. He's into amateur dramatics in a big way. I actually saw him in a production of *Aladdin* playing the Widow Twankey and I swear to God he was hilarious — but as Jesus Christ he was even better — obviously not in a hilarious way but ...

Laura I understand.

Jim Right. So Nick's line to me and my mother is coming up and I'm still really furious with her from the night before. "Woman, behold your son," cries Nick. (*Pause*) At the start I didn't know whether it was his great delivery or just thinking about my mother being my mother — but I started to cry. I'm crying really hard. People are thinking that this is wonderful. I completely upstage Nick's crucifixion and the night's suddenly about St John and whether he's going to be all right and if he'll have the strength to carry on and start and finish his gospel. But anyway! Anyway! Afterwards, and my mother is having a lemonade in the sacristy and I'm out of my lime robes and looking over at her. And I realize why I was crying back then. (*Pause*) I was crying because I know my mother doesn't like me. (*Pause*) If I really remind her of the man she hates, the man who left us when I was six — then maybe I should walk away too. But where to? Where do I go to?

A pause

Laura The rule in the room is we don't give advice. We just listen.
Jim OK.

A pause

So what about you? Do you have anything you want to share?
Laura I just listen.
Jim No problems?
Laura Of course ... but I prefer to listen to other peoples'.
Jim What do you get out of that?
Laura I'm not too sure.

A slight pause

Jim Knowing that there are other teenagers struggling probably makes
you feel better about your own problems.
Laura No.

A pause

Jim These are very strange places, aren't they? Like I said, I don't
know whether I should be really here. Whether it's that serious yet.
What do you think?
Laura As I said …
Jim "The rule in the room is we don't give advice." Fine. (*He sighs.
Pause*) Have you been to many suicide chatrooms?
Laura Yes.
Jim And do they help you?
Laura Who said I needed to be helped?

A pause

Jim Can I know your real name?
Laura You can call me Laura.
Jim But is that your real name?

Laura Maybe.

Jim What city are you from?

Laura It doesn't matter. None of that really matters. You just need to know that there's someone listening to you. That's enough, isn't it?

Jim I suppose.

A pause

Will we talk about something else, Laura?

Laura I don't talk, I listen. You talk.

Jim Talk about what?

A pause

Laura Tell me about the day your father went missing.

The Lights change

Music plays for some time. We watch the six do nothing. The music cuts abruptly

The Lights change; William, Jack, Eva and Emily are lit

William We need to set rules.

Emily Why?

Eva We don't use our real names. We don't say what schools we're from ...

William We know we're from the same area and that's enough. Just leave out the details. It gives us more freedom.

Eva Keeps it impersonal.

William I'll use William.

Eva I'll be Eva.

Jack I always use Jack.

Emily Emily.

Eva How do we know you're not two middle-aged men trying to get off chatting up two teenage girls?

William How do we know you're not two frustrated housewives trying to take advantage of two innocent altar boys?

Emily Are you altar boys?

Jack Are you desperate housewives?

Emily

Eva   } (*together*) No.

William

Jack

William Excellent.

Jack I was an altar boy.

William Oh, fuck.

Jack No, I quite liked it.

Eva How?

Jack When you're seven you've got a very simple idea of life and for a while, dressed in my altar boy's gown every Sunday, I really thought I was some sort of angel. I called myself "an angel-waiter".

Emily Angel-waiter?

Jack You see I believed in Adam and Eve and that God created everything in six days and that he had a rest on the Sunday. And I had this image of the church being like a restaurant/café for God to rest in ...

Eva Or a McDonald's?

Jack Exactly. And it was my job as an angel-waiter to serve him on his day off.

Eva So what does God eat?

William Chicken nuggets.

Emily laughs

Jack I was only seven.

Emily That's very cute.

Eva How long did you think this?

Jack Several months.

Emily And the whole altar boy thing?

Jack Four years.

Eva Four years?

Emily Are you religious now?

William I'd rather not talk about religion. You either do or you don't believe. End of discussion.

Eva (*to herself*) Dick.

William We're all around fifteen, sixteen. We're all middle class kids of varying wealth growing up in and around Chiswick. I think we know each other's views on boring issues like religion.

Emily Oh right. So what's mine?

William (*quickly*) You're disillusioned with the official Church and yet you remain spiritual and have defined your own personal religion based upon the simple idea — that people should be nice to each other.

A slight pause

Emily Bastard.

Eva laughs

William It's a cliché. We're all clichés ...

Jack Yeah, all people can be placed in little boxes like that.

William They can.

Eva So what are you?

William A pain in the arse.

Eva Apart from that.

William I'm a cynic. I'm an angry cynic.

Eva Very attractive.

William I'm not interested in being attractive. Why should I be?

Eva Because attractive people go further ...

William Yeah I think I glanced at that article in one of my sister's magazines ...

Eva People see a cynic as a black hole. They're nothing. While a person who might be attractive or charming ... Well, they're at the very centre of things — changing things — manipulating events. What are you but a bad smell?

William That's very kind of you.

Eva You know what I mean.

William You think I'm heavy-handed?

Emily You certainly sound that way.

Jack He's bloody opinionated.

William Well that's the name of this room, isn't it? "Chiswick's Bloody Opinionated"!

Emily (*groaning*) Christ.

William I'm at the age — we're all at the age when we have to stand up for something. To me it's not about making friends and going bowling and sitting in McDonald's bumming cigarettes and talking about the latest McFly LP — that's a waste of fucking time! Now's the time to be a pain in the arse and step away from other people. We're teenagers! That used to mean something. It was about revolution. Apart from the punks what have teenagers achieved in the last thirty years? Nothing.

Jack Did punks achieve something?

William They made their mark! They were angry and they showed it.

Emily My mother was a punk. We've got this photograph from 1979 and she's got a coldsore on her cheek the size of a tennis ball. Quite amazing.

Eva It was dirty work being a punk.

William Nowadays teenagers wouldn't go that far before cracking open their cleansers.

Emily Oh, definitely.

Jack I don't know about that. I cultivated a boil on my neck last year for a few weeks. My mother brought me to the doctor and I was gutted when he said he wouldn't lance it ...

Eva Aww...

Jack But he gave me this black plaster with this tiny hole in the middle. It sort of draws the pus out towards the little hole.

Eva Do we have —— ?

Jack So I'm watching television with my dad and my baby brother and above the telly I hear this noise. (*He makes a quiet splurting noise*) I swear to God it hit the wall behind me.

Emily That's disgusting.

Jack But it was a revolution!

Eva How?

Jack My body was revolting.

Eva (*slowly*) Oh, the comedy.

William But does anyone know what I'm talking about?

Emily Not really.

Eva Yeah, I do.

William Finally!

Eva I went on an anti-war march and for an hour or so I felt really good and I felt empowered. But it was just so small. In the great big scheme of my life it was just one hour of saying that I believed in something.

Emily Oh, yeah.

William (*to himself*) Oh, please.

Eva I suppose the rest of the time we're sleepwalking and waiting for something to happen instead of making something happen. It would be so great to accomplish something important. To have a cause.

Jack William wants to assassinate J.K. Rowling.

Emily and Eva laugh

William I was only joking.

Jack You talked about it for an hour last week in the Harry Potter Chatroom.

William It's not her personally — it's the idea of her — what she stands for.

Emily And what's that?

Jack William reckons children's writers simplify everything to keep children simple.

William They see us as a threat.

Eva Who do?

Jack Adults.

William It's like the adults support these writers to write these pointless stories of fantasy so that children have this cutesy warped idea of what life is about.

Eva So J.K. Rowling is the Field Marshal?

William She's the enemy. Not her but the idea of her. If I could kill the idea of her without getting her hurt I'd do it tomorrow.

Emily Are you actually a lunatic?

William I just want to do something important! It's frustrating.

Eva Would you ever kill anything, William?

William No. Any idiot can kill something. Where's the glory in that?

Jack Aren't you meant to say that each life is sacred?

Emily Exactly.

Eva That's crap.

William There are some people and life is just wasted on them. Terrorists, dictators, racists...

Jack PE teachers.

Emily laughs

William They don't do anything. They suck all the goodness out of living.

Jack Like William.

William Shut up.

Eva I think William just wants a cause. He wants to see that cause through. He wants to make a big statement.

William Yes, exactly. I want to make a big statement. Who doesn't? (*A slight pause*) Thanks, Eve.

Eva It's Eva.

William Right. Eva.

There is a long pause in which the four of them do very little

Jim Is there anyone there?

A Light comes up on Jim

Jim Are people still awake? Is this room really called "Chiswick's Bloody Opinionated"?

William We don't use our real names, names of schools, any details. It's enough that we know that we come from the same area.

Jim Right. I'll be Jim, then.

Eva Hallo, Jim, I'm Eva.

Emily Emily.

Jack Jack.

William I'm William.

Jim So what happens here? I don't know this place. What's up?

William Heated discussion. Chit-chat. Bullshit.

Eva We're looking for a cause? William wants to make a statement.

Jack We're all a bit frustrated.
Eva If you have any causes handy feel free.

A pause

Jim Can we talk about our problems here?
Eva Oh God.

A pause. William laughs a little

William Have you got problems, Jim?
Jim Yeah, I do.
Emily Are they big problems?
Jim Well I think so. Big to me anyway.
William And you want us to listen to these big problems and give
   you some advice?
Jack Jesus, William ... !

A pause

Jim Are you still there? Look I'll go to another room if you want.

William starts laughing to himself. A pause

William Jim?

A pause

Jim Yes?
William We're here to help you.

The Lights change

*Music plays. They do very little. Maybe they get up. The music cuts
out*

The Lights return to them

Jim So I've been bullied all the way through primary and now in secondary school. I'm very skinny and a bit funny-looking so it goes with the territory. You expect it. But I have bigger worries — deeper worries that I can't really explain. And that's tricky. And very recently I've started to feel, "What's the point? What's the point in everything!" But not in a moaning, teenagey way ...

William Your depression isn't pretension.

Jim How do you mean?

William You're genuinely depressed.

Jim One hundred per cent genuine! I'm not one of these people who keeps an altar to Kurt Cobain or anything like that. I actually can't stand Nirvana. I don't need their music to feed my depression. I can happily do it all by myself ...

Eva Obviously not happily.

Jim Yeah! Yeah "happily"'s the wrong word —but you know what I mean.

Jack What does depression feel like?

William It feels great, what do you think!

Jack No, I know it's crap ... I just want to know what it feels like to Jim.

A pause

William's face takes on a look of exasperation

William Well, Jim?

A pause

Jim It's like the whole world has turned into soup. Everything has the consistency of soup. And your insides and your heart ... Well, they just sort of ache — and it's like you're clogged up with about five sliced loaves of bread. It's exactly like that.

A slight pause

Emily Wow.
Jack Depression's like bread and soup?
Eva Shut up, Jack!
Jack I'm only repeating ...
Jim The food comparison probably doesn't work.
William Schizophrenics often say they feel like a mixed salad.

Eva, Jack and William laugh. Jim smiles

Emily You sound sweet. Do you have a girlfriend?
William Oh, wait a second! We're here to give Jim some advice ...
Emily I just wanted to know if you had anyone close to you. You don't have anyone in your family to talk to — so I thought maybe an understanding girlfriend would help you to...
William Jesus, Emily if you'd been listening to Jim for the last hour you wouldn't ask that. Jim doesn't have our normal teenagey problems. It's not a problem that can be solved by a quick feel outside the chip shop!
Eva He's different.
William Of course he'd love a girlfriend! But that can't happen 'cause he's dealing with just getting up in the morning and facing into another one of his shitty days!
Jim I'm not that bad ...
Eva Maybe think before you speak, Emily!
Emily Piss off!
Eva No, it's just bullshit! I expected more from you! You didn't strike me as some head-in-the-sand princess.
Emily I'm not like that!
William Selfish cow!
Emily Jesus, all I said was ——
William Jim has the courage to come into this room and open up and tell us all this pathetic crap. All you're asked to do is imagine that others can be different from you.
Emily You have no idea what I'm like.
Eva Well by a comment like that... like Jim could be cured by the heart of a good girl...
Emily I didn't mean...

William Sorry about this Jim...

Jim No really it's...

Eva I think we've all got a good impression of the type of girl you are, Emily!

Emily Fuck off!

Eva Living in a little suburban bubble. Small group of girlfriends who hang around after music lessons sniggering over copies of *Bliss*.

William They're all called Sarah, right. Sarah-Jane, Sarah-Marie, Sarah-Louise, Sarah-Anne...

Eva The hair-band brigade in your deck shoes and Lacrosse shirts ...

William What's the worst that's happened to you?

Jack Oh come on guys...

William Scuffed your chinos in the park? That night daddy didn't pick you up from Pizza Hut and you had to get the bus home!

Eva Or maybe when your pony had to be put down 'cause your big fat preppy arse was buckling its back ...

Jack Hoy!

William Shut up, Jack!

Emily I had anorexia, you know!

Eva So what!

William Weekend anorexia, was it? Bursting out of those chinos?! Had to shift a few pounds?

Emily (*to herself*) What?

Eva Anorexia's a status symbol for your type of girl. You wear your six months' anorexia like a badge of honour. You think it gives you an edge? It makes you a stereotype! That's why when someone talks to you about their depression you can bat it aside with that shit about: "If only you had a girlfriend you'd be feeling a lot better." Christ if we let you drone on you'd be singing, "Cheer up, Charlie".

William "Willy Wonka's Chocolate Factory" ... I hate that fucking film! Get out of here, Emily!

Eva We want people who are here for Jim.

Emily I'm here for Jim!

William Someone who understands his problem. Who gets the cause.

Jim What cause?

Emily What, Jim is your cause now?

William We're here a hundred per cent and on twenty-four hour call. Jim's feeling cut up over something and we're here to listen and advise him, understood?

Eva That's right.

William We don't need any chaff! Jim doesn't need some ex-anorexic-pony-rider whining little *TV Digest* sound bites!

Eva Put simply ——

William Piss off!

A pause. William and Eva laugh. Emily looks very upset

Eva Is she gone?

William Hardly matters.

Jack I thought we were supposed to be friends.

Eva Silly cow.

Jim Maybe she didn't mean what you think.

William There's no need to defend her, Jim. She's not needed.

Jack Anorexia's terrible. You shouldn't have said those things.

Eva Forget about her ... She's debris. We're here for Jim. What about you, Jack?

Jack Yeah, I suppose.

William A wonderful vote of confidence there ... Maybe a bit more conviction, Funny Man?

Jack Well, no offence, Jim — but we're your age ... Shouldn't you be taking advice from a doctor, maybe?

Jim Well, I was actually thinking ...

Eva Christ, Jack, that's so fucking cruel. Don't you get it? He doesn't have anyone. We're it!

Jack Look all I'm saying ...

William Jack!

A pause

Can we step into Kylie's Chatroom? I want to talk to you in private.

A pause

Jack OK.

The Lights go down on all but Jim and Eva

Jim That was all a bit weird.
Eva Well, you don't have to worry about that now.
Jim OK, then.
Eva So tell me about the day your father went missing.
Jim Well, it's quite important — shouldn't I wait for the two boys to
    come back?

Eva looks exasperated

Eva (*sweetly*) I'll get them my notes.
Jim All right then.

A pause

> Right, well, I'm six years old and my three brothers are going away
> with my mother for the weekend — a treat for something or other.
> My dad's staying behind and my mother says that he's to look after
> me. That it would be a chance for us to bond. So they're gone and
> me and my dad are sat at the kitchen table looking at each other. Like
> we're looking at each other for the first time, you know. He asks me
> what I want to do and straight away I say I want to go and see the
> penguins in the zoo. When I was six I was going through some mad
> penguin obsession. I used to dress up as a penguin at dinner times and
> always ask for fish fingers — stuff like that. If it wasn't penguins it
> was cowboys. Cowboys were cool. A penguin costumed as a cowboy
> was always a step too far, funnily enough. (*He laughs a little*)

Eva (*groaning; to herself*) Oh my God.
Jim So we go to the zoo and I wear my cowboy outfit — get my gun
    and holster, my hat and all that. We get the bus and it's sort of funny
    to see my dad on a bus and away from the house. We start to have this
    chat about when I was born and what a really fat baby I was — but
    how after a week or so I stopped eating any food and everyone was
    very worried. That he was very worried. That he was so happy when

I got better and they could take me home. (*A slight pause*) We're in the zoo and I go straight to the penguins. Standing in my cowboy gear — looking at the penguins — having such a great chat to my dad on the bus — it was a perfect childhood day. (*Pause*) He lets go of my hand and says he'll be back with my choc ice. And he goes. (*Pause*) He's gone. (*Pause*) I'm happy looking at the penguins but it's an hour since he's left and I go to look for him. I'm walking about the zoo and I'm not worried yet. And I don't talk to anyone. I leave the zoo and I go to the bus stop we got off at earlier. I get on the bus. I tell the driver my address. He asks where my parents are and I say they're at home waiting for me. I stay on the bus in the seat nearest the driver. After a while we end up at the end of our street and the driver says, "So long cowboy." (*He smiles a little*) He was nice. (*Pause*) I get the key from under the mat and open the door and go inside the house. And I'm alone there. I take off my cowboy clothes and hang up my hat and holster. It being Saturday night I have a bath and get into my pyjamas because my dad would have liked that. I have a glass of milk and some biscuits and watch *Stars In Their Eyes* 'cause that was his favourite programme on the telly. (*A slight pause*) It's getting dark outside and I start to worry. The house is feeling too big so I get my quilt and take it into the bathroom and lock the bathroom door and it feels safer with the door locked so I stay in there. And he's not coming back. (*Pause*) He's never coming back. (*Pause*) I stay there for two days.

Eva looks bored

Lights come up on William and Jack

William (*in private to Jack*) It will be a laugh. Right now we're all he has. We're there for him twenty-four-seven ... It will be a blast! Eva gets it, why can't you? He's our cause. Let's let him talk. Mess him up a bit. See how far he'll go.

Jack says nothing

Are you there, Jack? Are you with the cause, Jack? (*Calling in a "Mummy" voice*) Oh, Jack?

A pause

Jack What next?

William smiles

The Lights change. Music plays

They rearrange themselves so that Eva and William are sitting on either side of Jim, with Jack sitting just away from them. Eva and William produce small notebooks. Jim (in dumbshow) talks non-stop and they take notes

After one and half minutes the music cuts

During the following Eva and William read out their notes

Eva A lower-middle-class family with your mother having notions above her status. Hence the extra-curriculum activities. The rugby, the horse riding, the rowing classes …

William Et cetera, et cetera, et cetera.

Eva At the age of four and you realize that the children on your street laugh at your brothers for their aggressive social climbing ——

William —— and the people in the rowing club laugh at them for wearing the pikiest clothes.

Eva Your first feelings of anxiety when you understand that you are living in a family hated by everyone and that you are one of them.

Jim Right.

William You decide to stay indoors. But being the youngest brother to brothers built on the rugby field they adopt you as their plaything and later their punch bag.

Eva At the age of five you go back outside to play with the other children ——

William —— only to see that bonds of friendship have already been formed ——

Eva —— and there is little room for a small tubby toddler who has an unhealthy obsession for penguins.

William You are all alone but you do find a friend in … Ahhh?

Jim Timmy.

Eva (*sighing*) Little Timmy Timmons.

Jim Yeah.

William A tiny six-year-old with severe bronchial problems who has to drag an oxygen canister behind him. When the other children play road-football ——

Eva — you are watching Timmy's mother slap phlegm out of Timmy's chronic lungs and into a Tesco bag.

William Watching this at the age of six you have your first thoughts on your own mortality.

Jim True.

William One momentous day, your father leaves you in the zoo leaving the family in the shit.

Eva Your mother is forced into getting her very first job. She finds work in a petrol station, ending all her dreams of the posh life and throwing her into a depression eased only by ——

William — Gin and tonic — the tonic being ——

Eva — Valium.

William Your best friend Timmy dies, not from the tragic weakening of his lungs in the middle of the night ——

Eva — but a speeding Ford Mondeo which flattens his trailing oxygen canister and leaves Timmy walking zombie-like through the mean streets of Chiswick as the other children shout ——

William — "Spa-Boy!".

Eva The day of Timmy's funeral you take your first Valium. You are aged eight.

Jim Eight and a half!

Eva (*correcting her notes*) Eight and a half!

William You try to make contact with your dad by placing leaflets on lampposts but to no avail.

Eva You try to make friends with anyone you meet by ingratiating yourself to whatever they want you to be ——

William — but to no avail. You decide to retreat back into the indoors and your Neanderthal brothers' daily beatings.

Eva You hide yourself in books of the occult which leads to a period of bedwetting.

Jim Is that important?

Eva Oh, definitely!

William You briefly turn to religion and take part in a Passion play where you realise that you hate Jesus Christ only slightly less than you hate your mother, the Virgin Mary.

Eva At thirteen you read your first porn which only creates more of a distance between you and those girls you will never get to touch.

William You hate yourself and decide to stop communicating with other people entirely. You're life is directionless.

Jim (*almost hyper-ventilating*) Jesus.

Eva The next two years are a sad cocktail of home-made beer, the odd Valium and the odd shot of whiskey.

William Nights begin to take on a pattern of aggressive self-analysis until one night you're talking to an American bloke on the internet who's planning to kill himself. His unfortunate name is Chad.

Eva Like Chad and the others in the suicide club — you reach a moment of recognition. You are searching for that elusive purpose.

William A purpose. (*Closing his notebook*) Right.

A pause. From now on Eva and William are not reading from their notes

Jim (*sighing*) A purpose. Fuck. Fifteen years. It's so depressing.

Eva If it wasn't such a tragic life it would make a very funny musical.

William I don't think you've ever been given a chance. For some reason you're the one who always gets burnt.

Jim But why me?

William You can't take responsibility for what people have done to you or what people think of you, Jim.

Eva The reasons why people have done those things isn't something you have control over. "Why me?" is a pointless question. Stupid even.

Jim Right. Sorry.

William What you are feeling right now, this moment, that's all that matters. Concentrate on that.

Jack But try and think more positive …

Eva Oh, shut up, Jack!

Jack But fuck it guys, all this talk …

William Jack!

Jack No, this is just bullshit. You're just highlighting all the shit that's happened to Jim. Jim listen to me. Things have been hard, I can see that ...

William You don't care about Jim.

Jim Yes, I care!

William Why don't you tell him what you said to us earlier?

Jack What are you talking about?

William Be honest with him. Tell him.

Eva Tell him, Jack!

Jim What did you say, Jack?

Eva I told him about your dad and how he left you when you were a child and Jack started laughing.

Jack What?

Eva From the outset Jack's been saying that you sounded like a spoilt little twat who needed a kick in the arse.

Jim You said that, Jack?

Jack No!

William He can't be trusted, Jim. He's one of these hard-working lower-class types. Doesn't even live in Chiswick. He's a Brixton-boy or something. Apple of his mother's eye. He makes himself out to be everybody's friend. He's a backstabbing bastard.

Jack Fuck off ...

Eva Nothing worse than someone ashamed of their background, is there, William? Some eager beaver effecting a voice to get on.

Jack Oh Jesus ...

Eva Sitting around the dinner table looking at the dumb faces and cringing at the stupid chit-chat of family life.

William Can't you see him! The Little Lord Fauntleroy of Stockwell stuck in his bedroom and dreaming of escape.

Eva He thinks that way about his own family then friends must mean shit.

William He's got no friends. It's all virtual with, Jack. Can't have people seeing him for what he really is.

Eva What does Jim mean to the superior Jack, I wonder?

William Some whingeing twerp.

Eva Some middle-class quack.

William A gutless jibbering child.

Eva One of life's morons.

William A spoilt imbecile.

Eva A mollycoddled spastic.

Jack Jim, please ...

Jim Shut up, Jack!

Jack But this is ...

William Jack, you worthless piece of shit! Why don't you take your
    snobby elitist backside and just fuck off back downstairs to an evening
    of Pringles and Sky One!

Eva (*laughing; to herself*) Too good.

Jack (*snapping*) Fuck it!

The Lights go down on Jack

William So sorry you had to hear all that, Jim.

Jim And he seemed like such a good person.

William I know — and you think you know someone.

Eva Continue then, William.

A pause

William Jim?

Jim I'm listening.

William You have to focus on your anger and channel it into something
    that will get all those people in your past back.

Jim How do you mean?

A pause

How do you think you would hurt your mother for all those years of
neglect? All those years she treated you like nothing.

Jim Well I've been fighting her for so long now ...

Eva But she doesn't listen to you, does she?

Jim No, she doesn't. And it doesn't make me feel any better.

Eva So?

A pause

Jim I've been thinking about if she came into my room in the morning and if I had done something ... (*Pause*) Like maybe I've cut my wrists or taken pills or something ... I can imagine her face.
Eva Bitch.
William She'd be crushed. The guilt would kill her.
Jim Yeah, I suppose it would.

A pause

Jim But I don't know if I'm ready to do that.

William and Eva look irritated. A pause. William settles himself

William Jim?
Jim Yes.
William Me and Eva can't imagine what your life's been really like. It just sounds so...? So sad. Without hope, probably.

Eva laughs a bit

But we've been giving up our time and listening to you for the past few nights, haven't we?
Jim Yeah. And thanks, lads, really.
William I only want you to do one thing for me, all right?
Jim Yeah, sure, William. Whatever it is.
William I want you to ask yourself two questions before you go to sleep tonight. Do you have a pen and paper to write the questions down?
Jim (*producing pen and paper*) Emmm? Yeah, go on.
William Why is it people treat me like I'm nothing?
Jim (*writing; as he does*) Why is it people treat me like I'm nothing?
William If no one cares about my life why should I care?
Jim (*writing; as he does*) If no one cares about my life why should I care?

Jim finishes writing the questions then silently reads them back. Suddenly something's got his attention. He looks sharply to his l.

Jim It's two o'clock in the morning and my mother's outside hoovering the stairs and landing. Tonight my three idiot brothers called me a freak for not wanting brown sauce on my quiche. (*A slight pause*) I better go. Thanks guys.
William Sweet dreams.

Jim stands up and moves away from his seat

Eva He's ours.

Music plays; the Prodigy's "Smack My Bitch Up" screams along. William and Eva burst out laughing. The music ends abruptly

The Lights cross-fade to Jack, Emily and Laura

Laura The rule in the room is we don't give advice.
Jack He spoke about you. He spoke about this place ...
Laura I can't help him! So if you're not here for anything else ...
Emily But he might listen to you.
Laura If he's suicidal the last thing he needs is someone else giving their half-arsed opinions. It doesn't help, believe me.
Jack It's not like that. He's being talked into doing something ...
Laura I can't get involved! Look, what I do is sit here and listen to people my age who have these urges to hurt themselves. Most of the time they don't do anything. A lot of the time they just need to know that someone is listening to them because they either feel they don't have anyone or they actually don't have anyone. That's all I do!
Jack But right now the only people he has are two strangers who want to see him do something to himself.
Laura I don't go into other rooms any more. There's too much shit that goes on. People get hurt.
Emily Exactly.

Laura stands away from her seat. She's agitated. A pause

Jack Christ. Are you still there? Laura? Laura, please?

Laura If you want to pass on my e-mail to him it's laura15%@aol ...

Jack Oh for fuck sake! You don't have to talk if you don't want to. Just come and you'll see. If it gets too much you can always get out. We'll be right there with you.

Laura But who are you? How do I know I can trust you?

Emily I started a mathematics club in school called "The Brainiacs". I've never so much as looked at a boy. There's nothing I'd like more than to get out of this hideous body, to be able to forget the difference between common and natural logarithms ——

Jack Emily ... ?

Emily — to be able to surprise myself. Last night I had a dream and I swear to God I think I experienced my first orgasm. Today, in looking back over the details of the dream, all I can remember is Stephen Hawking asking me to change his batteries! Believe me, Laura, you can trust me! I am a trustworthy person. What we all need to do here is take our heads out of our arses and try and do fucking something!

Laura remains silent

Emily Are you there?!

The Prodigy's "Smack My Bitch Up" resumes from where it was cut

William and Eva place their seats to face those of Emily and Jack. Jim places his seat between those of the two groups. Lastly Laura places her seat next to Jim's. The whole six stand and look at each other like they're sizing each other up for the big showdown. Jack is the first to sit, then Emily, Laura, Jim, Eva and finally William. As William sits the music cuts out

The Lights change

Eva As little babies you can't do any wrong, can you, William? You're bloody perfect! All you do is eat, shit, laugh, cry, sleep, don't sleep but you're loved. And I suppose you're loved because your parents have this blank page, don't they? And all their hopes can be projected on to this beautiful little blob.

William And the blob can't disappoint because it's just a beautiful little blob. But of course that only lasts a few months until bang!

Eva Suddenly the blob's a little too hungry, a little too loud, a little less beautiful.

William And then it's a little toddler and its character is forming and it's only right to be a bit more critical now that it's a little toddler. Too quiet, too shy, too aggressive, can't stop eating, a little too cranky ——

Eva — blah blah blah blah blah blah ——

William Before you know it the toddler's ten years old and let's say that another baby is born.

Eva Oh typical!

William The ten-year-old is this big mouth to feed. This ever-growing child who disappoints, causes worry and sucks your money. Your parents' hopes are already on the next blob because at ten years of age a person is made, a character's developed.

Eva The damage is done.

William It certainly was with me.

Eva Now just imagine what the teenager means to its parents if a ten year old means that, Jim?

William Well, we're not a child, not an adult.

Eva *Not a Girl, Not yet a Woman.*

William Oh, Eva, please!

Eva Britney speaks the truth!

William A teenager is "a sub-person".

Eva Not that Britney used the lyric "sub-person" ...

William This hormonal mess. A boy-man, a girl-woman. We're like a bad experiment.

Eva So true.

William If God had really thought things through — we'd be babies born on the Monday and fully grown adults on the Tuesday, because everything else in between is this long list of fumblings, mistakes and bad skin.

Eva Oh the bad skin!

William The teenage years.

Eva And the voice we have, William.

William What voice?

Eva Any voice that hasn't been shaped by some shit children's writer or some draining pop star … If we do have an original thought — it's just seen as a joke, isn't it? It's a joke 'cause those adults who have lived through these years remember them with complete and utter embarrassment.

William It's not that we're misunderstood or not understood at all.

Eva No.

William They understand us completely because they've lived through these years and see it as their right ——

Eva As their adult duty!

William — to patronize us with the words, "Whatever you're going through, you'll get through it."

Eva "Now clean that bloody bedroom, bitch!"

William Your mother would use "bitch"?

Eva By fifteen you've realized that the individual doesn't mean shit and the average teenager is seen as the big embarrassing joke. We're all just folded up neatly and placed into a box marked, "The Awkward Years". But when you allow yourself to be summed up that simply — from fifteen onwards you will live the rest of your life through these different phases. You will be summed up into little boxes until they stick you in your final box and shove you in the ground. Guaranteed. Only a few teenagers make a stand. Only a few brave souls make a statement. Teenagers like you, Jim.

Jim Like me?

William I was thinking that Jim's depression allows him to see things clearer than us. He's been neglected by his family and friends so that maybe his isolation represents perfectly the average teenager's plight. It's like he's expressing important issues in a creative way. It's poetry. It's a metaphor, Eva.

Eva It's quite brilliant, Will.

William But you know, Jim, maybe the more public you make it the more of a statement you'd be making.

Eva What an excellent idea!

Jim How do you mean?

William Imagine all those forgotten teenagers you'd be speaking for if you killed yourself publicly. You'd be a hero. A legend.

Eva Very brave. Very romantic. Sexy even.

Jim Do it in public?

A pause

Jim I'm not too sure about that.
William Maybe show it over the internet then. Would it be easier in your bedroom?
Jim Yeah, I suppose.
Eva It sort of seems right that he remains alone. That people see him die like that.
William Well it's stronger, isn't it?
Eva Definitely.

A pause

Jim Well I'm usually alone anyway so... And for the past few weeks I don't like being out in public places so much. Seems easier if I do it here.
Eva Can you get a webcam to broadcast it?
Jim My brother Jonathan has one.
William Perfect.

A slight pause

Jim Of course he'd kill me if he found me using it.
William Well, we wouldn't want that to happen, would we?
Eva It sort of steals your thunder.
Jim Yeah.

William and Eva laugh

Laura Jim, this is Laura.

A pause

Eva And who are you?
Emily She's come in with us.
Laura I've spoken with Jim before. We know each other.
William You're a friend of his?

Laura Why exactly are you harassing him like that?

William We're here for Jim. Do you know what state he's in?

Laura I know he's not feeling well.

Eva What?

Laura He hasn't been feeling good about himself. He's lonely. He feels detached.

Eva He's suicidal! He's ready to take his life.

Jack Which is what you want!

William Oh, piss off, Jack!

Laura Why is it you're doing this?

William We're his friends.

Emily No, you're not.

William We didn't abandon him like you two. He came to us looking for advice and we've been making things clear for him.

Laura You're talking to him like there's no options. You're making him believe that there's nothing else. That suicide is some romantic gesture. Like one fifteen-year-old's death will be held up by other fifteen-year-olds and celebrated for something. Will make a big statement for all those "trapped" average teenagers! If you think of yourself as some blob who's moulded into this empty child and sent on a set pattern through life ... If you think that — it will happen.

William It will happen! Choices are made and choices will be made where you have no control. Your life is set!

Laura That's shit! Every single moment in life there's possibilities.

William gets up from his seat

William (*snapping*) Bitch!

Laura The statement being made is yours. But what are you saying, William? That you've got power? That you're smart enough to take advantage of someone vulnerable and talk them into the corner where they might kill themselves? And this is some joke to you two, right? Some big comedy. Because you can't see him it's easier. It's easier when you don't have to see a dead boy and just imagine it like you read it in a book or something. It's easier than murder, isn't it William, 'cause Jim's faceless to you — but it's just like murder. In these rooms words are power and you and that bitch have all the right words ...

William Eva, come on!
Eva (to herself) Ah fuck this.

Eva exits

William You've tried to kill yourself but chickened out, haven't you?
You think I'm going to allow Jim to be lectured by some whingeing
coward like you. Some New Age happy-clappy princess! Jim has
real problems.
Laura This isn't some competition about who's the most sad here!
And if you need to know, you dick, I have tried to kill myself! I did
slit my wrists. It did come from a very real place! But I'm happy I'm
alive. And some days are better than others and the future scares me
but I'm ready for the struggle! And I like the struggle! I like it a lot
more than being dead and stuck in the ground and watching over my
family and friends who I've torn apart. Stay alive and they can help
me! There's always a life!
William You're one of those sad girls who hangs out in suicide
chatrooms. Who just sits there like some black hole. All silent and
dumb and soaking up the sad stories. Wallowing in other people's
pain. What statement are you making, bitch? You talk about a life of
possibilities, choice, love, happiness ... but I bet you'd like nothing
more than a world of sad, morose fifteen-year-olds draining on about
their pathetic lives. Well, why not support those who want to kill
themselves? Why not allow them do it? They're like the front line,
aren't they? The public face of our gloom, printed in the papers and
shown on the telly! They need our support to do the brave thing — do
the decent thing. To get rid of the chaff and make a true revolutionary
teenager! So do the decent thing, you worthless cow! Next time don't
cry out to Mummy and Daddy! Just do it!
Jim (*quietly*) Stop.

A pause

I'm fifteen and my life is mine to do with it as I please.

A pause

Jim Five of us are from the same area. Tomorrow at one o' clock I want you to be at the McDonald's on the High Street. I want you to be there because I can't be in my bedroom any more. Maybe I'll do it quietly but I want you to see me do it.

A pause

Laura Jim, I'm still here to talk to.

A pause

Jim You know I don't think I can listen to any more talking.

A pause

Let's finish this.

Music plays; the beautiful "Dawn" by The Cinematic Orchestra ("Man with a Movie Camera" album), continuing under all of the following speech. On the screen at the back of the stage a film is projected, showing Jim's journey down the High Street and into McDonalds and all that happens there. The picture is fairly bleached and ghostly and, in its early stages, is all from Jim's point of view

Laura places a chair with its back to the audience, sits and watches the film

By the end of the first section of the speech Jim, in the film, has arrived at McDonalds and is sitting at a table

Jim (*to the audience*) It's funny but I slept well. Probably the best sleep I've had in months. I left the house with my bag full of stuff and there was no-one there. My mother was working her shift in the petrol station and my brothers were at this American wrestling thing that was happening in Earl's Court. I got the bus and there was this man with his young son which got me thinking about me and dad and the zoo and the cowboy outfit — and all that. Seemed appropriate that I would see them. Typical. In the bus I started to think about all those thousands of teenagers who kill themselves every year. Somebody would be killing themselves right now maybe — while a number of others would have it all planned out. And a lot of them are doing it because — they really are very ill. And some are doing it because they're alone — or maybe they're sad because someone hurt them somehow. There are so many reasons to do it. And I started thinking about all the families and friends who are left behind and the regret that must eat them up. It's all so quiet and violent. (*Pause*) I got off the bus and walked through the streets and imagined all the ghosts of the dead teenagers looking at me. And what were they thinking? And what would they say to me? It's like they all follow me down the High Street and into McDonalds. And they watch me buy some chicken nuggets and a Coke and find a table. And the angels see me taking out my camera.

The film captures William, Eva, Jack and Emily dotted around the restaurant, just faces in the crowd

We get a flash of a gun on Jim's table. It's a toy gun but at this point it reads like it could be real

In this room those angels are waiting for me. And I don't see myself as anything other than me. I don't imagine what I'm about to do is making a big statement or speaking out for millions of teenagers. I'm alone.

The camera finally rests on Jim sitting alone at his table. He has a bag with him

I give the camera to this ten-year-old boy to hold. I tell him to point it at me and the table.

During the following we see Jim, in the film, take things out of his bag: a cowboy hat, sheriff's badge, and holster. People around him start to look at him as he carefully gets into the outfit

There's no question but I've been very sad about things. And I'm probably like thousands of teenagers who get depressed. It's almost enough for me to know that someone is there for me and someone is listening. But I had to do something for me. I had to grow up fast when my father left and it's as simple as that. And I really miss him and I can't understand why he's gone. Something that simple can mess you up for a long time.

In the film Jim takes an iPod out of his bag with two little speakers

When you're six and wearing a cowboy outfit and looking at penguins you shouldn't be made to grow up so fast. But I was. And I tore myself up over it for years and tried to find answers, but honestly — what can a child do? (*Pause*) I just want my childhood back.

In the film Jim exhales sharply, puts his gun in his holster and quickly stands on the table. He presses the button on the iPod and the song "Rawhide" is heard through the speakers. He closes his eyes and just stays still. People around him are smiling and laughing. The film goes into slow motion as it moves around his still upright body, his eyes closed, a small smile appearing on his face. We watch him for some time until a security guard drags him down

The screen cuts; "Rawhide" cuts

Jim and Laura, sitting in their seats, look at each other. There is a pause

Laura Everything all right now?
Jim Yeah. (*A slight pause*) You?
Laura Yeah. (*A slight pause. A little hesitantly*) Thanks for sending the film, Jim. It was good. (*Pause*) It helped.
Jim Good.

A pause

Will we talk about something?
Laura (*smiling*) What will we talk about?

A pause. Jim thinks really hard

Jim Bunny rabbits.

They both smile

Music: Wheatus are heard singing "A Little Respect"

Jim and Laura, in dumbshow, talk about bunny rabbits during the first verse. It's a conversation we're not allowed to hear

From above, bubbles float down on them. Laura catches one in her hand

The chorus pumps in

Black-out

"A Little Respect" continues through the curtain call

FURNITURE AND PROPERTY LIST

On stage: Six identical orange plastic seats

Personal: **William**: notebook and pen
                Eva: notebook and pen
                Jim: notebook and pen

LIGHTING PLOT

Practicals required: nil
A bare stage. The same throughout

To open: Darkness

Cue 1	When ready *Bring up general lighting*	(Page 1)
Cue 2	Oompa Loompa song ends *Fade lights on all but* **William** *and* **Jack**	(Page 2)
Cue 3	**Jack**: " ... do my geography homework." *Cross-fade lights to* **Eva** *and* **Emily**	(Page 4)
Cue 4	**Jim** sits *Cross-fade to* **Jim** *and* **Laura**	(Page 7)
Cue 5	**Laura**: "Tell me about the day your father went missing." *Change lights*	(Page 11)
Cue 6	Music cuts abruptly *Lights up on* **William**, **Jack**, **Eva** *and* **Emily**	(Page 11)
Cue 7	**Jim**: "Is there anyone there?" *Bring up light on* **Jim**	(Page 16)
Cue 8	**William**: "We're here to help you." *Change lights*	(Page 17)
Cue 9	Music cuts out *Lights return to* **Jim, William** *and* **Eva**	(Page 18)

EFFECTS PLOT

Cue 1	**Eva**: "Murder" *Music*	(Page 7)
Cue 2	**Jim** sits *Cut music*	(Page 7)
Cue 3	The Lights change *Music*	(Page 17)
Cue 4	When ready *Cut music*	(Page 17)
Cue 5	**William** smiles *Music; play for one and a half minutes, then cut*	(Page 24)
Cue 6	**Eva**: "He's ours." *Music: "Smack My Bitch Up" by the Prodigy*	(Page 30)
Cue 7	**William** and **Eva** burst out laughing *Cut music*	(Page 30)
Cue 8	**Emily**: "Are you there?" *Resume "Smack My Bitch Up"*	(Page 31)
Cue 9	**William** sits *Cut music*	(Page 31)
Cue 10	**Jim**: "Let's finish this." *Music: "Dawn" by the Cinematic Orchestra*	(Page 37)
Cue 11	**Jim** presses the button on the IPod	(Page 39)

	Cut "Dawn"; play "Rawhide"	
Cue 12	Screen cuts out	(Page 39)
	Cut "Rawhide"	

Cue 13	**Jim** and **Laura** smile	(Page 40)
	Music: "A Little Respect" by Wheatus	

MUSIC COPYRIGHT

PROJECTION PLOT